D0606996

NIDO R. QUBEIN

Attitude

The Remarkable Power of Optimism

Edited by : Alice Patenaude
Cover and internal design : Brian Frantz
Photos: ShutterStock, ThinkStock, iStock & Fotolia

Published by Simple Truths, an imprint of Sourcebooks, Inc.
P.O. Box 4410, Naperville, Illinois 60567-4410
(630) 961-3900 • Fax: (630) 961-2168
www.sourcebooks.com

Printed and bound in China.

OGP 10 9 8 7 6 5 4 3

INTRODUCTION

If you want to reach for success in every area of your life, the most important asset you can have is a faithfully *optimistic, winning attitude*.

Literature and History Are Full of People Who:

Suffered from severe handicaps
Often had talents that were inferior to those around them
Sometimes lived in the worst of circumstances
Usually faced many defeats

Yet, many of those people are listed among the winners in life's Hall of Fame.

Why? What Made Them Achieve?

When others around them failed
When others had greater talents
When others had greater opportunities
When others often had far greater resources

The secret is this: They had *optimism* and developed a *winner's attitude!* Whether you reach success or failure in life has little to do with your circumstances; it has much more to do with your *attitude*…with your *faithful courage*…with your *choices*!

You see, non-achievers *blame* their circumstances; winners *rise* above their circumstances. Some concentrate on the blank wall that boxes them in; winners always look for a way to get under it, over it, around it, or through it.

At High Point University, we create an environment that encourages our students to adopt a winning attitude—to be extraordinary! Our goal is to *weave* students into our HPU family, rather than to *weed* students out of the system.

Over many years of consulting with business organizations and association with individuals of all ages and at all levels of accomplishments, I have been fortunate to accumulate a treasure trove of wisdom about developing an optimistic winner's attitude. Much of it has found its way into books I have written or into videotapes or audiotapes I have made, as well as through speeches, seminars and newsletters.

In this book, I've tried to refine this accumulated wisdom into short entries that can be read quickly, absorbed easily, and applied successfully. It is content that I share in courses I lead for freshmen and for seniors at High Point University and now, I'm happy to share it with you. Whether you are a student in college or an executive of a major organization, I hope you will find this book a pleasant source of inspiration and advice.

Nido Qubein

"*Pessimism* leads to weakness,
optimism to power."

~ William James

How Do You Get Out of Bed?

There are two kinds of people in the world—positive people and negative people. Optimistic, positive people spring out of bed in the morning and say, "Good morning, Lord!" Pessimistic, negative people pull the covers over their heads and moan, "Good Lord, it's morning again!" Which kind of person are you?

"*I* can't change the direction of the wind, but I can adjust my sails to always reach my destination."

~ Jimmy Dean

Optimist or Pessimist?
It's Your Choice

*W*hether you are an optimist or a pessimist, the choice as to how you will be in the future is yours, and yours alone. If you are like the people who aren't happy unless they are miserable, you can stay that way. If you want to be joyful, enthusiastic, and excited about life, you *can* be, regardless of your circumstances.

"*Y*ou were born to win, but to be a winner,
you must plan to win, prepare to win,
and expect to win."

~ Zig Ziglar

Develop a Winner's Attitude

*S*uccess is mainly a question of attitude. If you go into an undertaking expecting to succeed, the odds are great that you'll succeed. If you go in fearful of losing, you're more likely to lose.

If two evenly matched football teams clash on the field, which is likely to win?

In all likelihood, the school with a winning tradition. That's because its players expect victory. If a team has a losing tradition, its players are often surprised by victory, which is why they have mediocre seasons even when they're loaded with talent.

It's been said that the late Bear Bryant, legendary football coach at the University of Alabama, went into each game with a winning attitude that was worth at least one touchdown for the Crimson Tide.

Cultivate a winning attitude. It will sustain you even when the odds seem stacked against you.

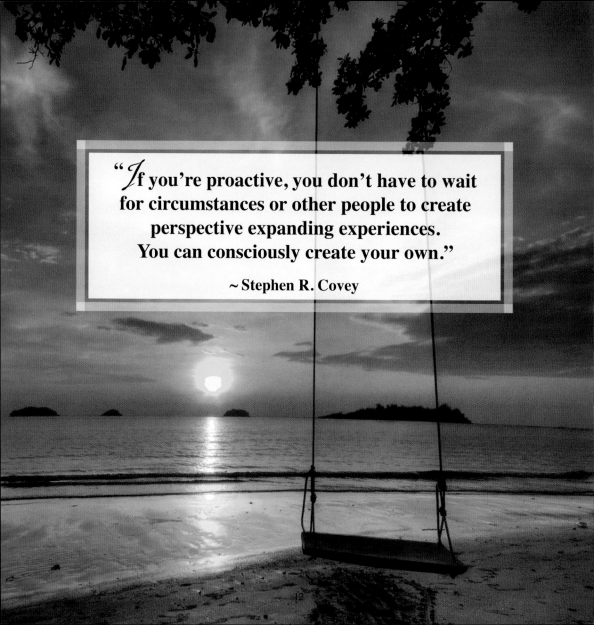

"*If* you're proactive, you don't have to wait
for circumstances or other people to create
perspective expanding experiences.
You can consciously create your own."

~ Stephen R. Covey

Winners Are Proactive

*W*inners are proactive, not reactive. They *create* new circumstances, not simply *respond* to circumstances.

Reactive people are likely to go through life complaining about their circumstances. They focus on things they can do nothing about and ignore the things that are within their circle of influence.

Proactive people look for ways to succeed in spite of any circumstances.

If you live in a northern state, you can stay inside during the winter and complain about the snow and the cold. Or you can take up snow sledding and skiing.

If you live in a large city, you can complain about traffic congestion and the cost of parking, or you can car pool or use public transportation.

If you're a high school graduate, you can complain about the scarcity of jobs for people without college or technical training, or you can go to college and receive an education.

If you don't like the way things are, complaining won't change them. Action will.

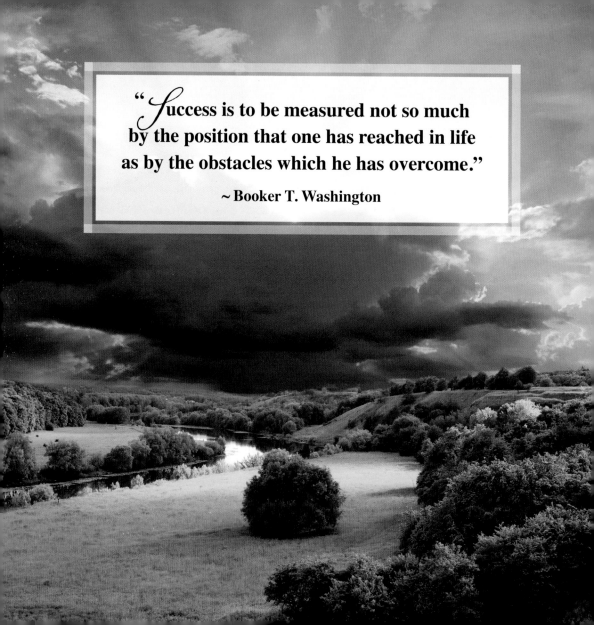

"*Success* is to be measured not so much by the position that one has reached in life as by the obstacles which he has overcome."

~ Booker T. Washington

Own Your Challenges

*Y*ou can maximize your chances of success by assessing, categorizing and prioritizing your challenges. Ignore those challenges that are unlikely to affect your success and happiness either way. Look for ways to adjust to those situations that you can do nothing about. Focus your efforts on the things you can change.

"*It* is hard to fail, but it is worse
never to have tried to succeed."

~ Theodore Roosevelt

Don't Be Afraid of Risk

*S*uccess in almost any undertaking requires that you engage in risk-taking, and with each risk comes the element of fear. How you respond to the fear makes the difference between success and failure. If you cower before it, running for cover at the first hint of disaster, you will fail. If you meet it boldly, letting it motivate you to action, you will succeed.

The issue is not risk avoidance—that doesn't solve the problem—the issue is risk management. Successful people don't avoid risks. They learn to manage them. They don't dive off cliffs into unexplored waters. They learn how deep the water is, and make sure there are no hidden obstacles. Then they plunge in.

"The purpose of life
is a life of purpose."

~ Robert Byrne

Pursue a Purpose Bigger Than You

*P*eople with a winner's attitude know that fame and fortune are not the only measures of success. Public recognition and money are only superficial ways of keeping score. What drives the winners to put forth Herculean effort, to bounce back from failures and defeats, to overcome handicaps, to battle discouragement and fear, is the knowledge that they are involved in a purpose that is bigger than they are.

Success focuses on three Fs:
-Fans
-Fame
-Fortune

Success is focused on tasks, even goals.

Significance also focuses on three Fs:
-Faith
-Family
-Friends

Significance focuses on purpose. When you set your sights on living a life of significance, you use your talents to make this world a better place and work to plant seeds of greatness in the lives of those around you.

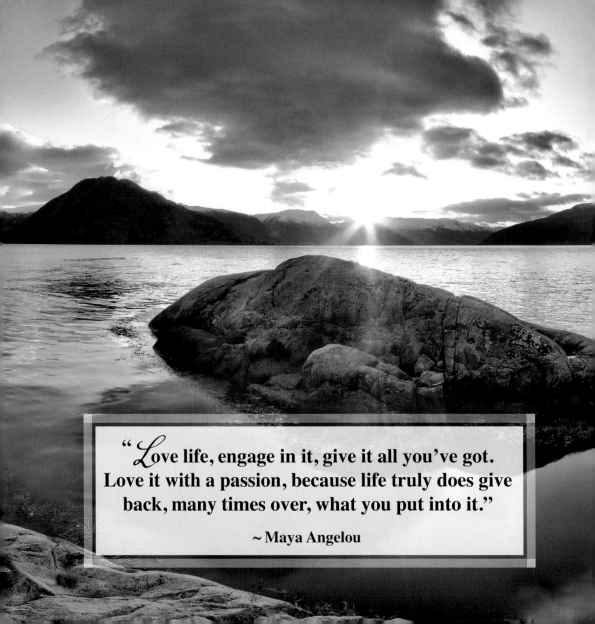

"*Love* life, engage in it, give it all you've got. Love it with a passion, because life truly does give back, many times over, what you put into it."

~ Maya Angelou

The Doctrine of "And Then Some"

*H*ave you ever eaten until you were so full you felt that you couldn't eat another bite? But then when the server came around with a tantalizing dessert, you were able to make room for it, weren't you?

You ate all you could hold "and then some."

Have you ever been in a race and come to the point that you thought you couldn't run another step? Then you saw a rival overtaking you, and you forced yourself to pick up the pace and run to the finish.

You gave it all you had "and then some."

Has your schedule ever been so full that you knew you couldn't find time to do anything else? And then the boss came in and said, "I'd like for you to take on one more project this month. There's a nice bonus in it for you if you can handle it."

You did all the work you could handle "and then some."

When you're sizing up your capacities, allow for the "and then some." The "and then some" provides you with positive stress that enables you to meet the challenge—and then some.

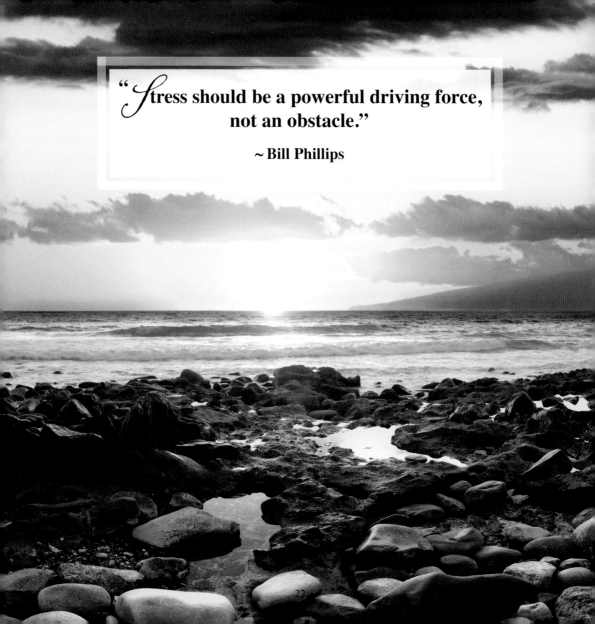

"*Stress* should be a powerful driving force,
not an obstacle."

~ Bill Phillips

Put Good Stress into Your Life

*S*tress gets a bad rap around the workplace, but you should know that there is good stress and there is bad stress.

Good stress can be used like the tension in a bowstring. Unless you stress the bow and the string, your arrow won't fly straight to its mark. Good stress is fruitful friction. It allows you to produce the results that you're aiming for.

A person who is experiencing no stress is also experiencing no challenge. And people who are not challenged will not exert themselves to succeed. Unchallenged people are bored and unmotivated.

Challenged people are excited and ready for action. They're like a talented, well-trained team going into a championship game. The challenge of winning fills the team members with an exciting tension that puts the edge on their performance, causing them to play at their best—and win.

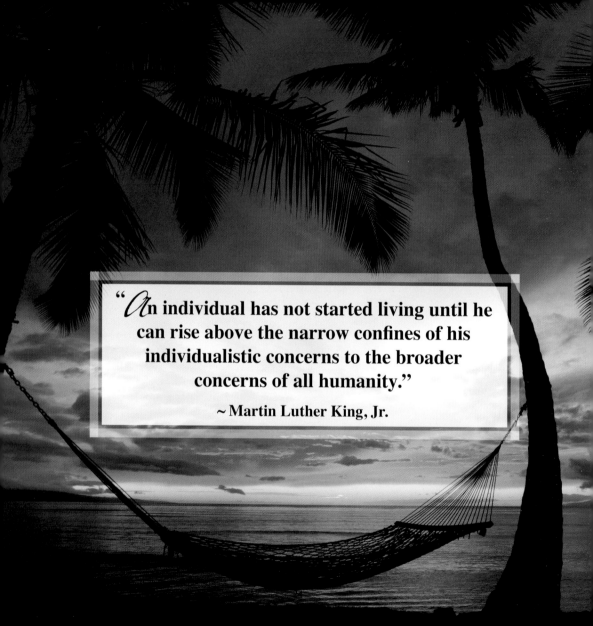

"An individual has not started living until he can rise above the narrow confines of his individualistic concerns to the broader concerns of all humanity."

~ Martin Luther King, Jr.

Winners Are Part of All Humankind

*S*ome see themselves as doing a job. Winners see themselves as a part of all humankind and their work as their contribution to a better world. George Bernard Shaw, the great English playwright, put it this way:

"I am convinced that my life belongs to the whole community and as long as I live, it is my privilege to do for it whatever I can, for the harder I work the more I live. I rejoice in life for its own sake. Life is no brief candle for me. It is a sort of splendid torch which I got hold of for a moment, and I want to make it burn as brightly as I possibly can before turning it over to future generations."

"*T*he best thing about the future is that it comes one day at a time."

~ Abraham Lincoln

Accept the Gift of the Moment

*T*he pessimist has screened out all of the exciting gifts that the present moment promises to bring, while the optimist is ready and eager to receive those gifts. The pessimist is either longing for a better moment, which may some day come, or reliving a more pleasant moment that is long gone. But the optimists are willing to trust in their plans for the future and in their ability to carry them out. They are willing to savor the memories of the past. Most of all, they are alert to the opportunities that each moment has to give.

"The secret of getting ahead
is getting started."

~ Mark Twain

The Future is the Place to Build

*Y*ou can't take charge of your life without an awareness of where you've been, where you are, and where you are going. But you can't build your life on the past. The past is gone. Nor can you allow your destiny to be limited by present circumstances. The present is fleeting. The only place left to build your life is in the future.

You can let the future happen, or you can create it. You create it by forming a clear, vivid picture of what you want and fixing your mental and emotional eyes on that picture. Let it become your vision, and it will draw you toward fulfillment.

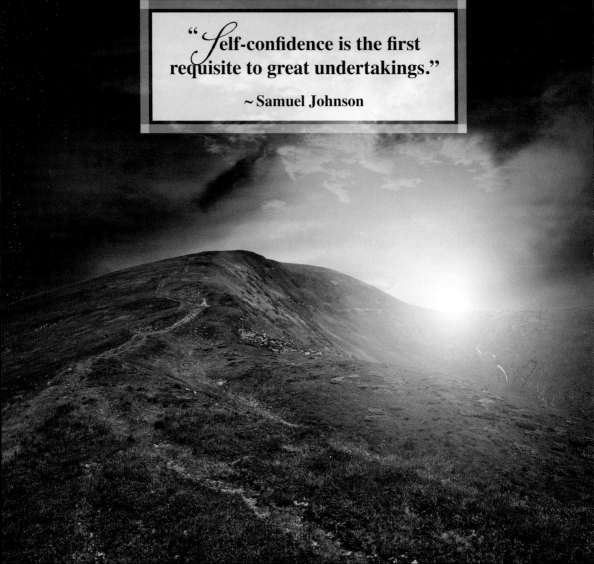

"Self-confidence is the first requisite to great undertakings."

~ Samuel Johnson

Have Confidence in Yourself

Self-confidence is often little more than a feeling, way down in the pit of your stomach, that you can do something that seems impossible. But as you respond positively to that little feeling, it grows and grows until it reaches full bloom in concrete action.

Sustainable confidence comes from competence and leads to commitment.

"Unless commitment is made,
there are only promises and hopes...
but no plans."

~ Peter Drucker

Decisions and Commitments

A decision is made with the brain. A commitment is made with the heart. Therefore, a commitment is much deeper and more binding than a decision.

Commitment involves feelings as well as thinking. It is the result of a well-documented formula: Thoughts plus feelings equal action.

Everything you do has to be born in the brain as an idea. That idea gives birth to a feeling. You act on the basis of the feeling. Therefore, your actions turn your thoughts into reality, once you have been motivated by your feelings.

The deeper and more intense your feelings, the more powerful the motivation to turn thoughts into action.

The thought creates a vision. The feeling makes the vision glow. Action brings the vision to life.

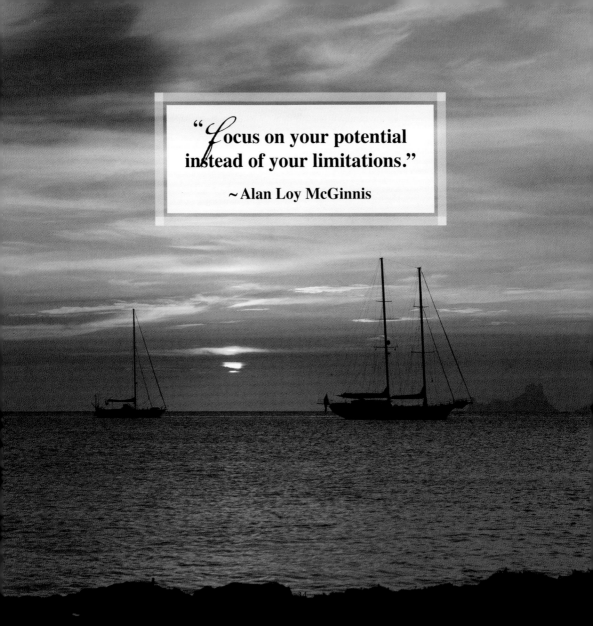

"*Focus* on your potential instead of your limitations."

~ Alan Loy McGinnis

The Most Valuable Person on Earth

*N*obody on earth is more valuable than you are. Your life is as precious to you as the greatest people's lives have been to them. And your estimate of your self-worth is the only estimate that counts. What other people think about you is your reputation. What God knows about you is your character. What you think about yourself represents your true worth. Thomas Edison's teachers thought he was just another hard-of-hearing, slow-witted kid. Edison knew better and he showed them.

You have abundant potential. All you need to do is to convince yourself that the potential is there. And then execute with faith and with courage.

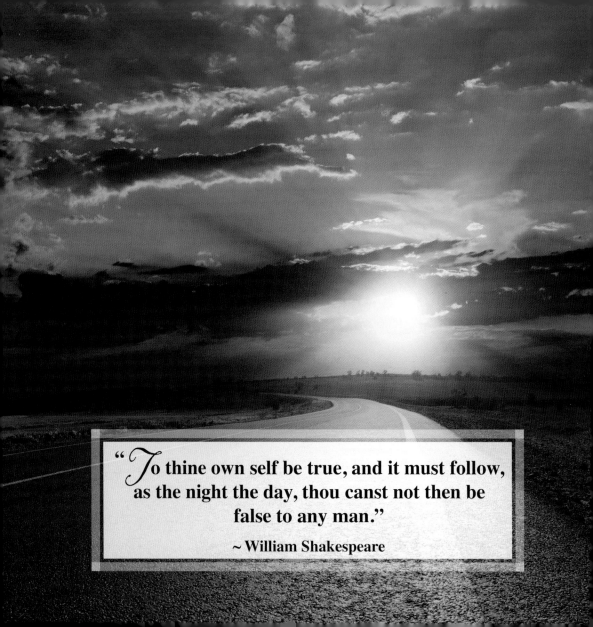

"To thine own self be true, and it must follow, as the night the day, thou canst not then be false to any man."

~ William Shakespeare

Always Be Yourself

A sign I spotted in a rural North Carolina store provided sound advice: "Be who you is, because when you is who you ain't, you ain't who you is."

A short adjective for people who try to be who they aren't is "phony." Nobody likes a phony. Be yourself, but be your **best** self.

Remember: Others value authenticity, even ahead of charisma.

"Happiness is not a goal; it is a by-product."

~ Eleanor Roosevelt

Value People, Not Things

People who are happy and successful learn to value people and to use things. People who are looking for something to make them happy, somehow never find it. Yet those who find a way to be happy while they are looking for something good, benefit in two ways. Not only are they usually happy while they are looking, but also they typically find what they are looking for. "He only is advancing in life whose heart is getting softer, whose blood warmer, whose brain quicker, whose spirit is entering into living peace," said John Ruskin.

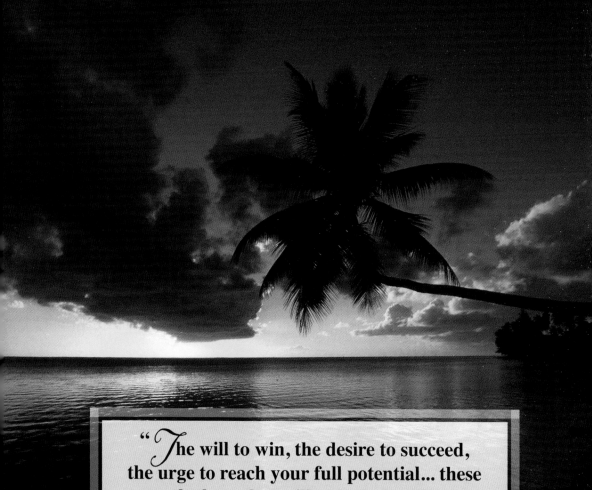

"The will to win, the desire to succeed, the urge to reach your full potential... these are the keys that will unlock the door to personal excellence."

~ Confucius

Use Your Power to Create

The human mind, coupled with an indomitable spirit and a miraculous physical body, is capable of creating in a way that is unknown anywhere else in the universe. Even when a physical body is limited in certain key areas, the human mind and spirit can break free to create in the most amazing ways.

If you would reach your full potential, cultivate all of the creative urges within you, and respond to the sensitivity that cries out for expression. Develop your best and most useful skills to their maximum level.

"*L*et no one ever come to you
without leaving better and happier."

~ Mother Teresa

42

Help Others Feel
Good About Themselves

*P*eople who have positive self-esteem tend to be genuinely helpful to other people. In fact, the two tendencies go together so well that it is hard to tell which produces the other. It is probably a little bit of both. Those who feel good about themselves long to help others feel good about themselves. The more they reach out to help others, the better they feel about themselves. Only the insecure, the frightened, the people with low self-esteem approach life with an attitude that says, "It's every person for himself or herself." Sadly, they find only more insecurity and lower self-esteem.

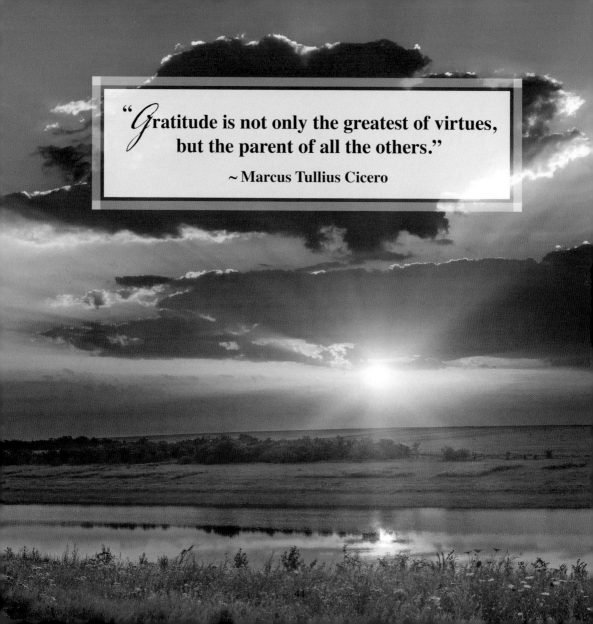

"*Gratitude* is not only the greatest of virtues,
but the parent of all the others."

~ Marcus Tullius Cicero

Be Grateful

Gratitude does not come easily for most people, because focusing our attention on what we want or need is easier than acknowledging what we have received. If you would build and maintain a healthy balance in your relationship with yourself and others, develop an active sense of gratitude. Don't whine.

Remember: Whining is the opposite of thanksgiving.

"Happiness depends upon ourselves."

~ Aristotle

Attitude Makes All the Difference

*P*eople with bad attitudes do not usually feel very good, about themselves or anyone else. Even when they're having a good time, they are not happy. They think to themselves, "This won't last." They can come up with too many reasons not to be happy.

With a good attitude, you don't dwell on the bad aspects of your life. You allow yourself to enjoy the good times. With a bad attitude, you waste good moments worrying about the past or dreading the future.

"The only difference between a good day and a bad day is your attitude."

~ Dennis S. Brown

Keep Your Lenses Clear

*S*uccessful people perceive the world neither through pink lenses nor gray ones. They prefer clear lenses that portray the world as it is, because that's the world they must deal with.

If you're looking at a gray reality, don't despair. Just shift your attention to another part of the picture. There's a bright side to almost every situation. Find it and focus on it.

"*A* positive attitude causes a chain reaction of positive thoughts, events and outcomes. It is a catalyst and it sparks extraordinary results."

~ Wade Boggs

Replace the Negative with the Positive

*T*aking the positive view requires more than simply casting out negative thoughts—although that is an important part of it. Positive input must replace negative thoughts. In fact, the quickest way to cast out negative thoughts is to feed enough positive thoughts into your mind that there is no longer room for the negative thoughts. People who take the positive view basically see the world as a good place. They actively look for the good in other people and situations, and they act with hope and faith.

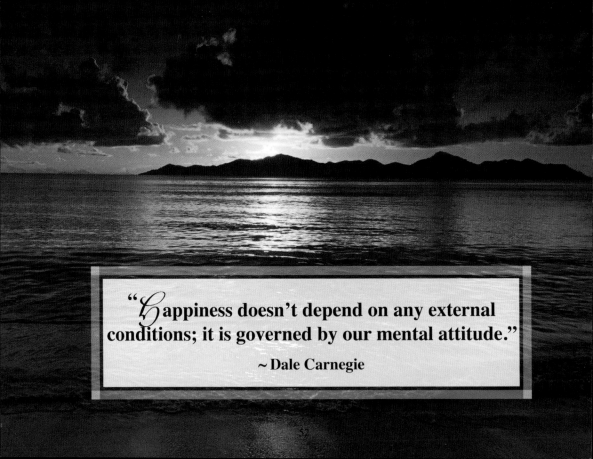

"Happiness doesn't depend on any external conditions; it is governed by our mental attitude."

~ Dale Carnegie

To Change Your Attitude, Change Your Mind

A change of attitude is like changing your mind. You just decide you are going to change the way you see things. You can't just pretend you have a good attitude. You have to have a good attitude.

You have to look at the bright side of situations, the good side of people—including yourself—and the positive side of negative events.

It's all a habit, really. Good habits are hard to develop but they are easy to live with. Bad habits are easy to develop but they are hard to live with. Develop good habits.

"We cannot solve our problems with the same thinking we used when we created them."

~ Albert Einstein

In the Long Run, Problems Look Smaller

*C*ultivate the art of looking at events in their proper relationship to your whole life. Often something appears for the moment to be a tragedy, but it becomes only a minor annoyance when taken in the context of your total life.

"*Y*ou are the same today that you are going to be in five years from now except for two things: the people with whom you associate and the books you read."

~ Charles Jones

The Power of Positive Influences

*S*urround yourself with positive influences. When you are surrounded by negative thinkers, images, or materials, it is easy to get bogged down in hopelessness.

Read inspiring books and magazines. Listen to motivational recordings and speakers. Attend positive-thinking seminars or programs. Make it a point to read or watch or listen to something positive and inspiring at least once every day.

Associate with positive people. Look for friends who feel good about themselves, people who have the attitude of gratitude. People who need to tear down others are not happy with themselves and are not good for you or your attitude.

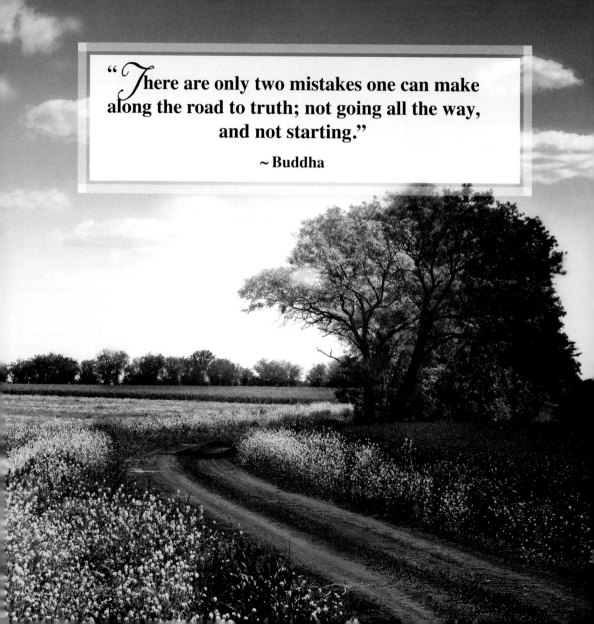

"There are only two mistakes one can make along the road to truth; not going all the way, and not starting."

~ Buddha

Mistakes are Seldom Fatal

$\mathcal{L}$earn to hold your mistakes and failures in proper perspective. The key lies in tying your sense of personal security to something deeper than immediate success. You can build and maintain your self-confidence by balancing your failures and mistakes against your long-term goals, your underlying purpose in life, and your inherent worth as a human being, rather than against their immediate consequences.

No mistake you could ever make would strip you of your value as a human being. Most mistakes detour you only slightly on your road to fulfilling your purpose in life. Mistakes are seldom fatal. It's your attitude toward mistakes that can cost you. Those who can come out of each mistake or failure better equipped to face the future are able not only to salvage self-confidence, but also to build it even stronger.

"To make mistakes is human;
to stumble is commonplace;
to be able to laugh at yourself is maturity."

~ William Arthur Ward

Don't Let Mistakes Get You Down

*T*ake a positive view of mistakes. If you goof royally, don't beat up on yourself. Congratulate yourself on the lesson you learned. Tell yourself, "I'll know not to do that again," and build on that knowledge. Know the difference between productive failures and non-productive successes.

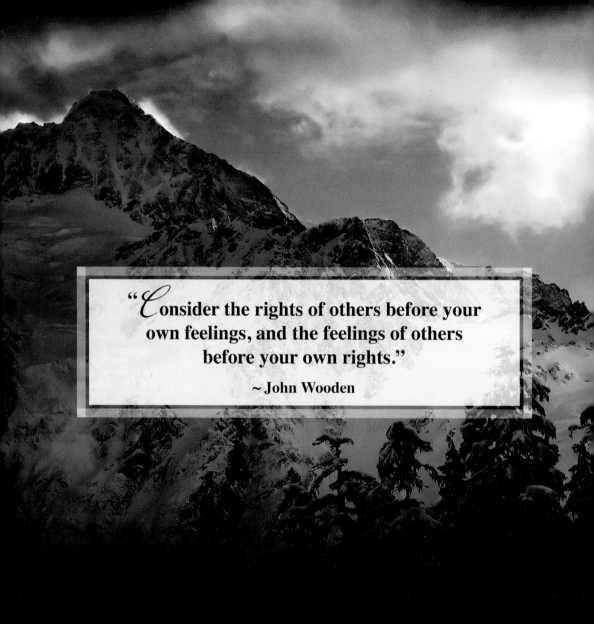

"Consider the rights of others before your own feelings, and the feelings of others before your own rights."

~ John Wooden

Wrap Yourself Around Others

*I*f you want a formula for becoming miserable, the first rule is to think only of yourself. People who think only of themselves, and what they want, find it hard to be happy with anything they get. For them, gaining the cooperation of the others who are so vital to their success is almost impossible. Many of their personal relationships are frustrating and disappointing.

"*Whether* you think you can
or think you can't – you are right."

~ Henry Ford

Feel Your Way to Confidence

*O*ur emotions are our least dependable, and often our most deceptive, sensing devices. What the wise old masters have told us in a thousand ways boils down to this: It is easier to act your way into feeling the way you want to feel than it is to feel your way into acting the way you want to act. In other words, master your feelings; don't let them master you.

"*Initiative* is doing the right thing without being told."

~ Victor Hugo

Avoid "Gotta-Do" Thinking

*M*any people live in a musty world of "gotta" and "oughta."

They are always telling themselves, or others, that they've "gotta do" this or they "mustn't do" that.

They live in a world of "should." When they don't do what they feel they should do, they feel guilty.

When others are told what they've "gotta do," they feel resentful. You ought to avoid "gotta do" thinking.

"How wonderful it is that nobody need wait a single moment before starting to improve the world."

~Anne Frank

Positive Attitude Should be Passed Around

I tell our students at High Point University that a positive attitude is like love in at least one respect: The more you give, the more you get. It does you absolutely no good to harbor all those good feelings inside yourself. The strength of a positive attitude comes from spreading it around.

Think of a time when you have helped someone see the positive side of a problem. Didn't you feel good about being able to help out? Sometimes an encouraging word is the best help you can offer to someone. So don't disregard the power of sharing positive thinking.

"To change what you get
you must change who you are."

~ Vernon Howard

Create a New Script

To seize the day, you have to make an irrevocable commitment to act. You do this by wiping the slate clean, creating a new script, and embarking on a course from which there is no turning back. What's past is past; what's done is done. The important thing is what you can do now to achieve the future you want. This requires a willingness not only to accept change, but to pursue it proactively.

"You can do anything you decide to do."

~ Amelia Earhart

Your Circumstances Are Not Your Prison

*W*hen you create a vision for the future, don't limit yourself to the things you think are achievable, given your present circumstances. If you're hungry, you want food, regardless of whether there's anything to eat near at hand. Your hunger will focus your mental and physical faculties on the task of finding food—and you'll probably find it. Think of the times when you've wanted to buy something but didn't have the money. If you wanted it badly enough, you found the money, one way or another.

It's that way with a vision. Without a glowing vision, you'll regard your desirable future as unattainable, and you won't focus your efforts on attaining it. You will be imprisoned by your circumstances.

"Man is not a creature of circumstances," said British statesman Benjamin Disraeli. "Circumstances are the creatures of men."

A vision bypasses circumstances. It finds a way around them, over them, or under them. Or it rearranges the circumstances. One way or another, it will take you toward your objectives.

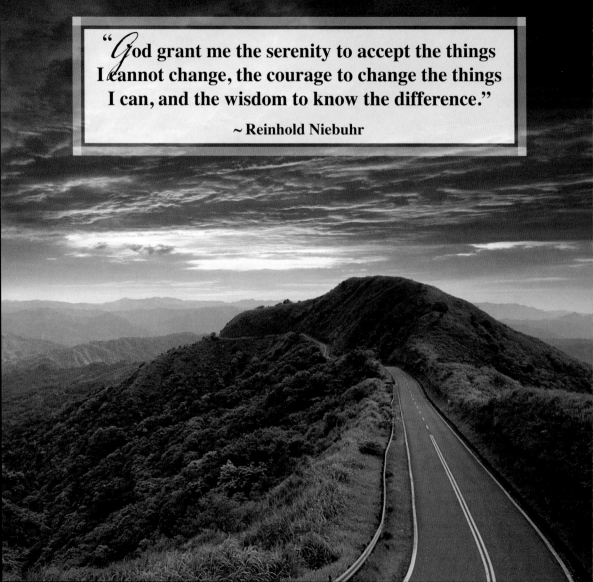

"God grant me the serenity to accept the things I cannot change, the courage to change the things I can, and the wisdom to know the difference."

~ Reinhold Niebuhr

You Can't Fix Everything

*S*ome things within your circle of concern are beyond your control. If you're middle-aged and beyond, you can't recapture your youth.

The things you've done and said in the past can't be undone or unsaid. So no matter how much you may regret them, there's nothing you can do to change history.

Some things are products of your heritage. You can't change your ethnic background, your gender or your height. If you were born with a tin ear, you might be able to master the techniques of the piano keyboard, but don't expect to achieve greatness.

Some things are beyond the range of effective action for you. You can't do a great deal about the national debt. You can't bring democracy to the Chinese mainland. And you can't change the climate in Fairbanks.

So it's a waste of time to worry about these things. Concentrate on the things you can do something about. You do have influence over your own finances, and you can vote for candidates who can influence national policy. If the weather doesn't suit you, you can wear clothes that are appropriate for the climate you're in, and you can heat or air condition your home to the temperature you prefer.

"*People* with goals succeed
because they know where they're going."

~ Earl Nightingale

Mobilize Toward Your Goals

*T*o make motivation pay off, you have to mobilize all of your resources in the direction of your goals. If you profess to be a positive thinker but have no aim in life, you're just spinning your wheels. What good is all the energy in the world if you have nowhere to go?

Mobilizing yourself involves deciding what you want, then determining what will get you what you want.

"*L*ife is a sum of all your choices."

~ Albert Camus

You Are the Product of Your Choices

At convocation each year, as we welcome more than a thousand first-year students to our university campus, I remind them and their families that we can't grow by repeatedly following prescriptions. We can grow only by making new choices. We are the sum total of the choices we have made in the past. We can change what we are in the future through the choices we make today. Choose well.

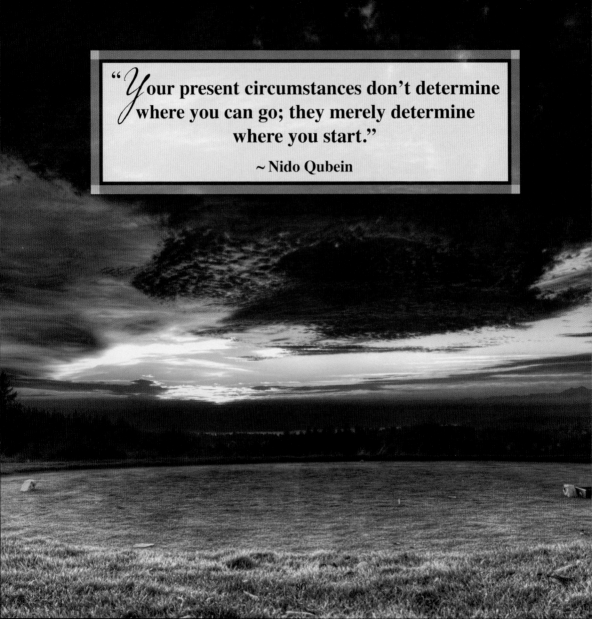

"*Y*our present circumstances don't determine where you can go; they merely determine where you start."

~ Nido Qubein

Play the Hand You're Dealt

*A*ccidents of birth are beyond your control. If you were born into a poor family without the means to send you to an Ivy League boarding school, you can't go back and trade your parents in for a set of millionaires. If you were born with a physical disability, you can't trade your body in for a better model.

But remember that the cards you're dealt are less important than the way you play your hand. Circumstances may be beyond your control, but you have full control of your responses to circumstances. The history books are full of success stories about people who focused their energies on the things they could do rather than the things they couldn't do.

It's not what happens to you that matters. It's what you do about it.

"*It's* wonderful what we can do
if we're always doing."

~ George Washington

Find What You Do Best— And Do It Heartily

If you want the kind of happiness and deep personal satisfaction out of life that circumstances cannot destroy, search until you find what you can do best, what no one could pay you money not to do, what you would gladly pay for the privilege of doing. Then do it with all that is within you. Your passion will lead you to success and significance.

"*E*ach person must live their life
as a model for others."

~ Rosa Parks

The Self-Confident Focus on Goals

*P*eople who have strong self-confidence tend to apply their personal power to useful goals. They let others talk about their abilities and deeds. They concentrate on goals, not activities. And they freely express admiration and appreciation to others.

It is enough for them to know the value of their goals and to believe in their abilities to reach those goals. They are far more concerned that their actions speak louder than their words.

"Some things are out of your control.
You can make it a party or a tragedy."

~ Nora Roberts

Things We Can't Control

We cannot always control what others do to us.

What happens to us.

Where we are born.

What physical challenges we have.

How much money we start out with.

What others expect of us.

How high our IQ is.

"Each of us has the freedom to choose
how we will respond to the circumstances
in which we find ourselves."

~ Nido Qubein

Things We Can Control

*E*ach of us can, and does, control how we react to what others do to us.

How we cope with what happens to us.

How well we use the physical abilities we have.

What we do with the resources we have been given.

How we respond to the opinions of others.

Whether we can, or will, live up to others' expectations.

What we do with the IQ we have.

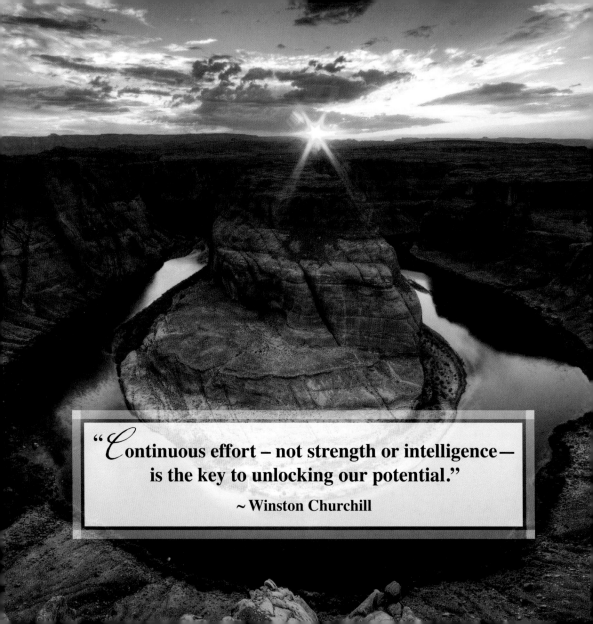

"*C*ontinuous effort – not strength or intelligence—
is the key to unlocking our potential."

~ Winston Churchill

Most Limitations are Artificial

*M*ost of the limitations that keep us from realizing our full potential are artificial. They are imposed on us by circumstances or by other people. Artificial limitations include:

Our age (we're "too" old or "too" young);
Empty pockets;
Past failures;
Troubles and pains;
The shortsightedness of those around us;
Lack of education;
Fears;
Doubts.

"*Life* has no limitations,
except the ones you make."

~ Les Brown

The Real Limitations

*P*hysical barriers and disabilities are not the real limitations that rob us of our freedom to make the best of what we have and of what we are. The real limitations have to do with the way we see ourselves and the world around us. Our attitudes hold us back from becoming all that we were created to be.

These real limits include:

A negative outlook on life;
Excuses we offer;
Wasting of precious time;
Pettiness;
Inflexibility;
Feeling sorry for ourselves;
Worry;
Procrastination;
Laziness;
Lack of self-discipline;
Bad habits.

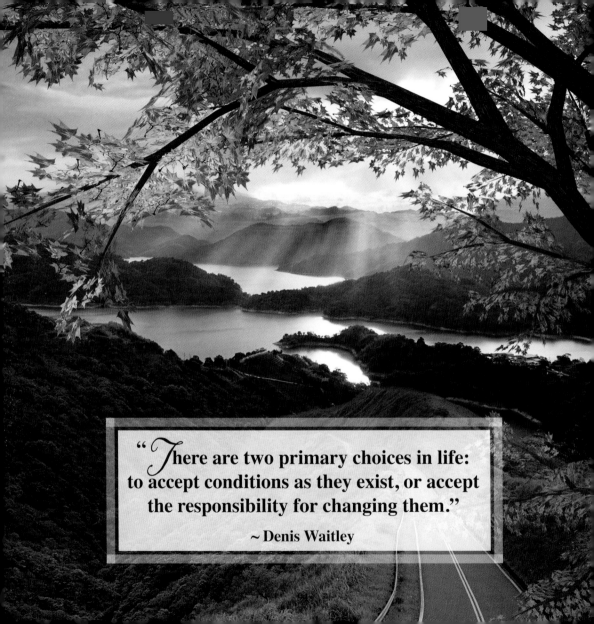

"There are two primary choices in life:
to accept conditions as they exist, or accept
the responsibility for changing them."

~ Denis Waitley

Use Your Freedom of Choice

*W*e talk a lot about freedom these days, but rarely do we exercise our most precious freedom. We all have a type of freedom that we seldom use in a purposeful way. You won't find it in the Bill of Rights and the Declaration of Independence only hints at it. No document of any nation anywhere in the world clearly spells it out. That's because no nation can give it to you, and no nation—no people—can take it away from you.

This freedom is equally available to all people regardless of race, religion, sex, economic status or circumstance. It is available to the prisoner, the invalid, to the poor, to the victim of discrimination, to the timid—even to the person who lives under a repressive regime.

What is this most basic freedom? Each of us has the freedom to choose how we will respond to the circumstances in which we find ourselves.

Life is a giant smorgasbord of choices. Yet here we stand, with our small plates that can hold only so much. Freedom demands that we make choices.

"*You* must be the change
you wish to see in the world."

~ Mahatma Gandhi

Look for Things You Can Make Better

Make it a habit to go about every day looking for things that you can change for the better. It may be something as simple as a minor change of routine. It may be a new hairstyle or a new approach to your wardrobe. It may be a different route to work.

One rule of thumb holds that when you've done something the same way for at least two years, there's probably a better way of doing it.

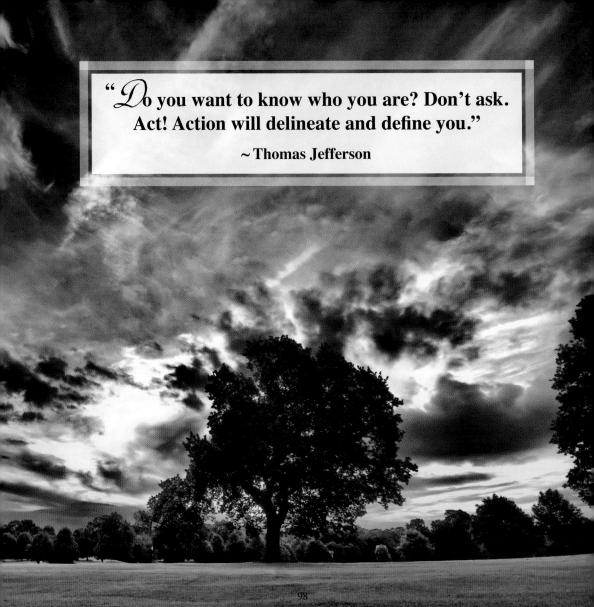

"Do you want to know who you are? Don't ask. Act! Action will delineate and define you."

~ Thomas Jefferson

Look to Yourself for the Answers

*P*eople who enjoy mental and emotional balance are self-reliant and self-determining. They don't blame their troubles or shortcomings on any person, circumstance or system.

They look within themselves for answers as to how things got to be the way they are and how things can be changed for the better.

They know that if they don't accept responsibility for their own circumstances, nobody else will. They will graciously accept help, but they are far more concerned with giving it. They make their decisions based on their own values and judgments. They work toward their own goals and live up to their own standards, respecting the views of others but refusing to be controlled by them.

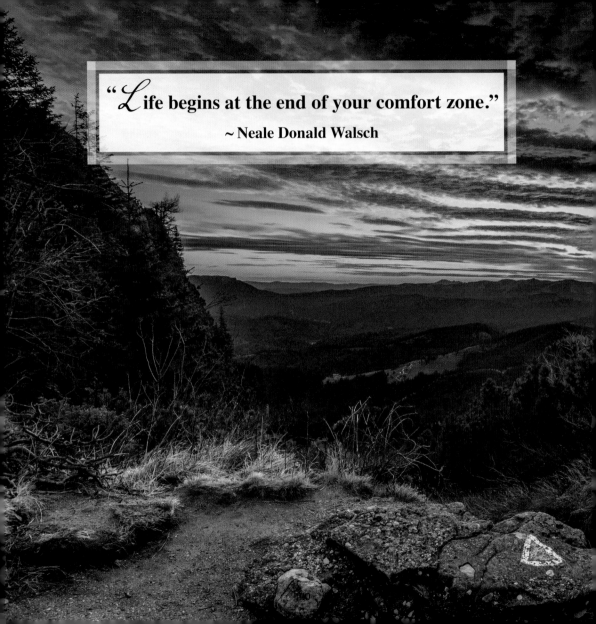

Venture Out of the Comfort Zone

*M*any people are not willing to pay the price to be successful. Maybe that's why so many withdraw into a "comfort zone." They long for a place to rest, a place to be safe, a place to be comforted and coddled.

But comfort zones are like caves:

Their darkness makes it hard to see.
Their stagnant air grows stale and becomes hard to breathe.
Their walls box us in.
Their low ceilings keep us from stretching to our full height.

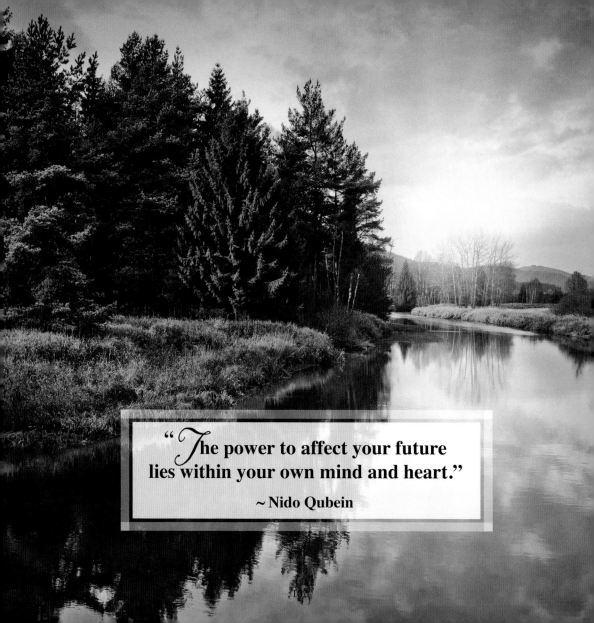

"The power to affect your future
lies within your own mind and heart."

~ Nido Qubein

Maturity Puts Mind Above Emotion

*A*lthough maturity involves many things, it certainly includes taking charge of our lives with the mind—through a series of rational decisions—rather than allowing our emotions to rule us. Perhaps this explains why boredom is such a problem in our society. People with adult bodies and minds who are still ruled by their emotions can never find enough fun and entertainment to satisfy their cravings. Jesus, the wisest teacher who ever lived, said that people's lives do not consist of the things they possess. If you're ever bored or dissatisfied with the way your life has been so far, maybe it's time to face up to the fact that you were born to be a winner. Stop following emotional whims; decide what you want, decide what you must do to obtain it, then act on your decision.

"*Those* who bring sunshine to the lives of others cannot keep it from themselves."

~ James Matthew Barrie

Don't Just Act Friendly; Be Friendly

*I*t isn't enough to act friendly. You have to be friendly. That means that you have to cultivate a genuinely positive attitude and a genuine concern for others. If you simply wear friendliness as a mask, the first stressful situation will unmask you and people will spot you for a phony.

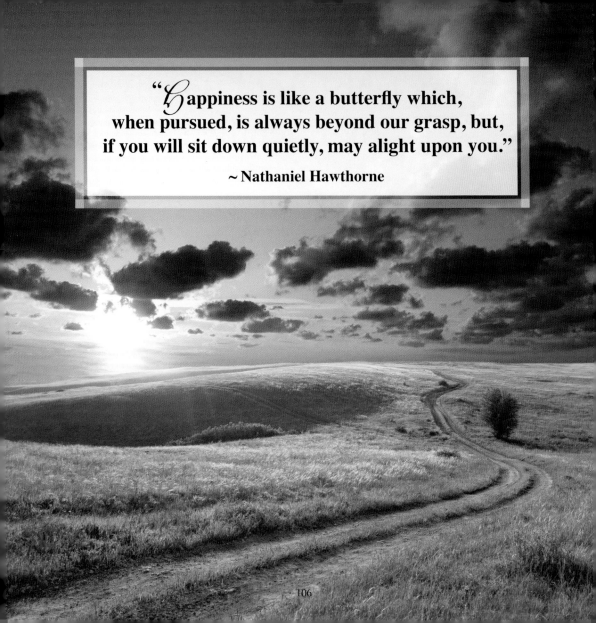

"Happiness is like a butterfly which, when pursued, is always beyond our grasp, but, if you will sit down quietly, may alight upon you."

~ Nathaniel Hawthorne

Stop Chasing That "Magic Moment"

One classic myth is that a person will "find" happiness at a future time—a "magic moment"—and usually in a distant place. Yet, as psychiatrist Victor Frankl said, "The search for happiness is self-defeating." Those who spend their lives searching for happiness never find it, while those who search for meaning, purpose and strong personal relationships find that happiness usually comes to them as a by-product of those three things.

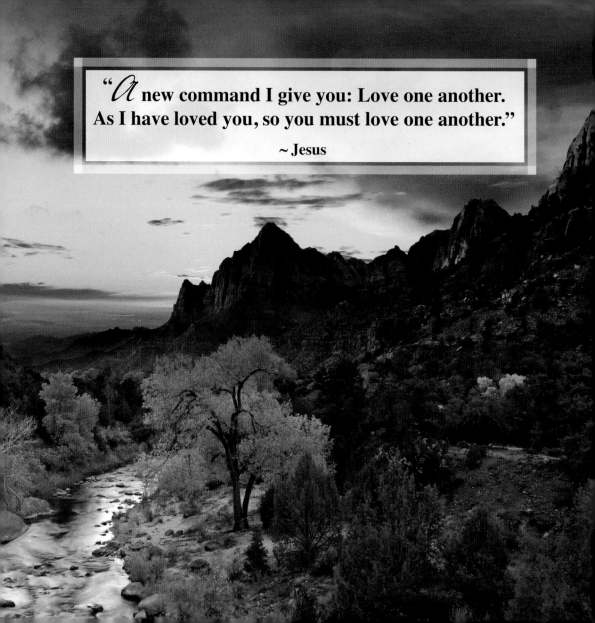

"*A* new command I give you: Love one another.
As I have loved you, so you must love one another."

~ Jesus

Use the Most Powerful Force in the Universe

*O*f all the human abilities, love is the most noble. It is by far the most powerful force in the universe. Love moves the spirit to create, the mind to think, and the body to perform. Hate may be a strong force, as are self-centered egotism and fear. However, nothing can lift you to the heights enjoyed by those who respond to the love within and the love from others. Only love can make all your success worthwhile. Whatever else you cultivate, cultivate love. Only when you love and are loved can you reach your full potential as a human being.

"The world spins, but not around you!"

~ Jasper Comstock

Soft-pedal the "I" Key

*N*obody likes to work around self-centered people. They're the people who always seem to turn the conversation toward their views, their virtues and their accomplishments. Or they constantly harp on their aches, their pains and their problems. They act as if they sit at the center of the universe, and everything revolves around them.

This self-centered attitude can be self-deceiving. People who see themselves at the center of the universe often believe that everyone else thinks the way they do. This can lead them to think that their way of thinking is the only valid way of thinking. Such an attitude closes the door to a lot of constructive and creative ideas.

"One of the most sincere forms of respect is actually listening to what another has to say."

~ Bryant H. McGill

Listening is Absorbing

*L*istening is to hearing what speaking is to talking. Hearing is the natural response of your ears to sound. But listening is using your ears and your mind to absorb and understand what the other person is saying.

You hear the noise of traffic. You hear the background music in an elevator. You hear the jet as it goes over your head.

But you listen for the sound of a ping in your engine. You listen to the cry of a baby to determine whether it's a cry of distress or a cry for attention. You listen when someone is giving you directions. And you listen when people tell you what's on their minds.

"*L*ife is either a great adventure or nothing."

~ Helen Keller

Don't Sit on the Sidelines

*L*ife should be an adventure, to be savored from beginning to end. It is a game of constantly changing odds, constantly developing challenges, constantly opening opportunities.

To win it, you have to play it. Sitting on the sidelines won't do. Even after you've achieved all you ever hoped to achieve, it's no time to stop living.

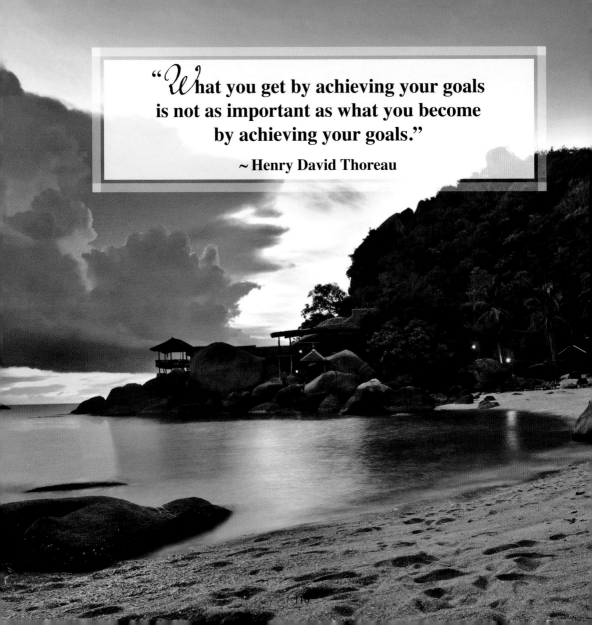

"*What* you get by achieving your goals is not as important as what you become by achieving your goals."

~ Henry David Thoreau

Goals Keep You Young

*O*nly when your memories are more important to you than your goals are you old. People who live on past glories, and who fail to keep their self-confidence growing, find that they gradually lose the faith they once had in their abilities. Without new challenges, they develop what someone has called "hardening of the attitudes."

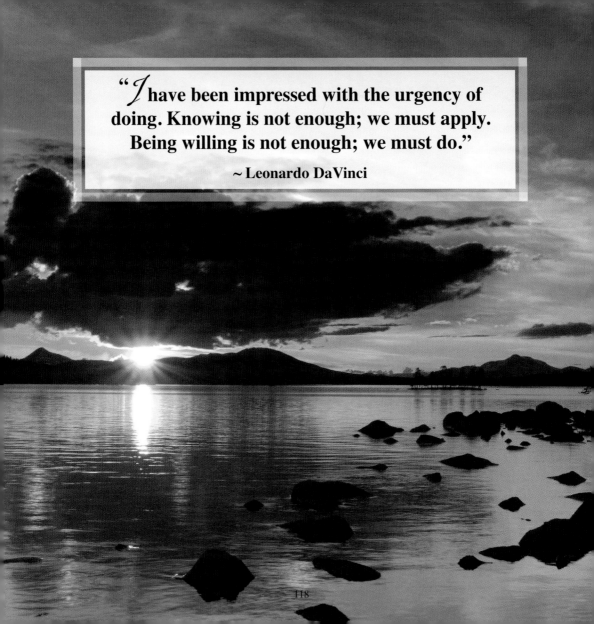

"*I* have been impressed with the urgency of doing. Knowing is not enough; we must apply. Being willing is not enough; we must do."

~ Leonardo DaVinci

View Problems as Opportunities

*I*f you could view your life as you do a highway from an airliner, many of the detours and curves would make more sense. The value of taking the long view of life is that it enables you to see problems as opportunities, passing up the fun-for-the-moment to pursue a worthwhile goal.

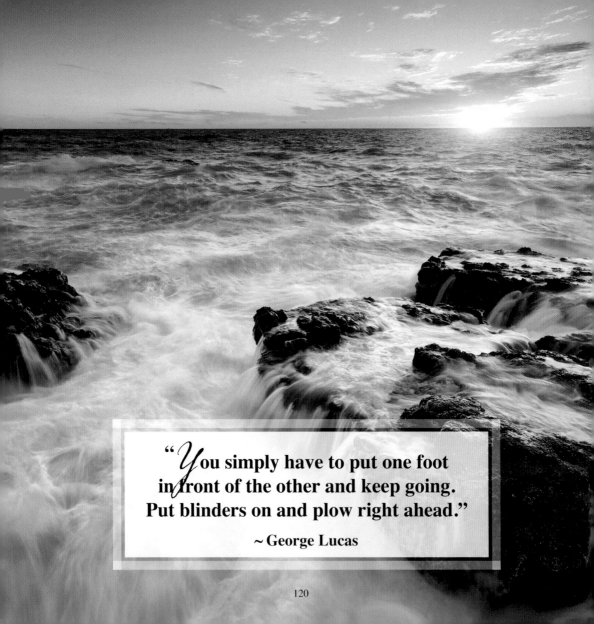

"*You* simply have to put one foot
in front of the other and keep going.
Put blinders on and plow right ahead."

~ George Lucas

Keep Moving

*M*ake inertia work for you. "There is a condition or circumstance that has a greater bearing upon the happiness of life than any other," said John Burroughs. "It is to keep moving." He compares our lives to a stream of water. "If it stops, it stagnates."

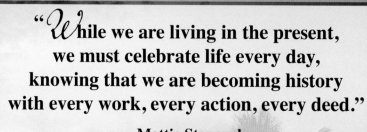

"*While we are living in the present,
we must celebrate life every day,
knowing that we are becoming history
with every work, every action, every deed.*"

~ Mattie Stepanek

This Is Your Life

*S*ome years ago, each week on a popular TV show called, "This Is Your Life," guests would be invited to participate in recreations of the special moments of their lives. I would like to suggest to you that today, this moment, this is your life! The only moment in which any of us ever lives is now. We may pretend that we live in the past, or we may imagine that we live in the future, but the only moment we ever live is this very moment—the now!

"The remarkable thing is,
we have a choice everyday regarding
the attitude we will embrace for that day."

~ Charles R. Swindoll

You Can Live Every Day of Your Life

*T*he law of inertia holds that a body at rest tends to remain at rest, and a body in motion tends to remain in motion, at the same speed and in the same direction, unless acted upon by an outside force.

With one major difference, that law applies very well to the pattern of our lives.

People who are successful tend to remain successful.
People who are happy tend to remain happy.
People who are respected tend to remain respected.
People who reach their goals tend to go on reaching their goals.
So what's the major difference?

In physics, inertia is controlled by outside forces; but the real changes in the directions of our lives come from inside us. As William James said, "The greatest discovery of my generation is that a person can alter his life by altering his attitude of mind."

You can live every day of your life. You can be alive to the tips of your fingers. You can accomplish virtually any worthwhile goal you set for yourself.

ABOUT THE AUTHOR

Dr. Nido R. Qubein came to the United States as a teenager with limited knowledge of English and only $50 in his pocket. His inspiring life story is one filled with both adversity and abundance. It is through the lens of his life's journey, that one appreciates his current role as an educator, philanthropist, and passionate advocate for the development of future leaders.

Dr. Qubein has served as the seventh president of High Point University since 2005, leading the university through an extraordinary transformation including huge increases in undergraduate enrollment, increasing the number of faculty from 108 to 236, and the construction of many new buildings on campus. Under his leadership, three academic schools have been added so far—the Nido R. Qubein School of Communication, the School of Health Sciences and the School of Art and Design. In addition, HPU's rankings moved up from #17 to #1 in Regional Colleges in the South in "American's Best Colleges 2013" by the *U.S. News & World Report*.

Prior to accepting his role as the president of High Point University, Dr. Qubein served as chairman of a consulting firm with clients in business and professional services. He is the recipient of the highest awards given for professional speakers including the Cavett (known as the Oscar of professional speaking), the Speakers Hall of Fame, The Horatio Alger Award for Distinguished Americans, The Order of the Long Leaf Pine (North Carolina's highest civilian honor) and Sales and Marketing International's Ambassador of Free Enterprise. Toastmasters International named him the Top Business and Commerce Speaker and awarded him the Golden Gavel Medal. He served as president of the National Speakers Association which has a membership of 4,000 professionals and is the founder of the National Speakers Association Foundation where the highest award for Philanthropy is named for him. He has been the recipient of many honors including the Ellis Island Medal of Honor, DAR's Americanism Award, and induction into Beta Gamma Sigma, the honor society for business leadership.

Nido Qubein's business experience led him to help grow a bank in 1986 and today he serves on the board and the executive committee of BB&T, a Fortune 500 financial corporation with $185 billion in assets and 35,000 employees. He is also chairman of Great Harvest Bread Company with 218 stores in 42 states and serves on the board of La-Z-Boy Corporation, one of the world's largest and most recognized furniture retailers. He serves as a director of DOTS, a national chain of 450 women's apparel stores and is a former trustee of the YMCA of the USA, which oversees 2,600 YMCAs across the country.

Dr. Qubein has written a dozen books and recorded scores of audio and video learning programs. He is an active speaker and consultant addressing business and professional groups across North America. You can reach him at nqubein@highpoint.edu or visit his website www.nidoqubein.com.